AF374800

This book belongs to:

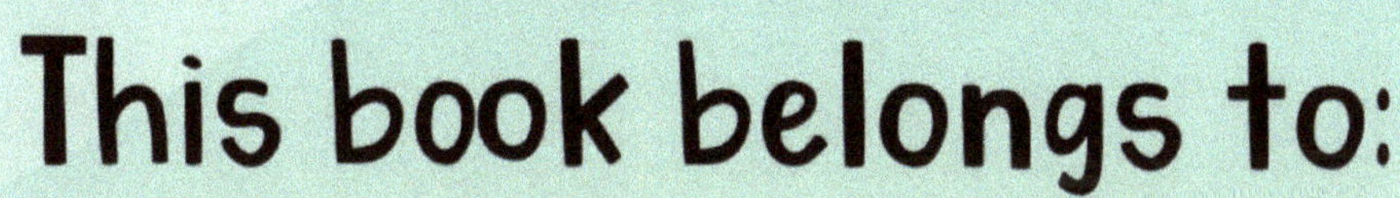

____

Copyright©2022 by Shamaya Raphael

www.babyshamaya.com

Dedication

This book is dedicated to everyone who needs a little boost in their confidence, self esteem, self worth and self love. Thank you for all who is and has been a big supporter in my journey. Big thanks to my Mom, Dad, Siblings, Aunties, Uncles, Cousins, Grandmas and Friends.

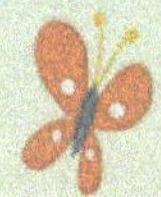

It all begins with me.

I love me, from the top of my head to the tip of my toes.

I am creative.
I am unique in every way.
I am perfect just the way I am.

3

I am loving, kind, and patient.
I am beautiful inside and out.

5

I am strong. I never give up.
I am O.K. with being me.

I smile because I am blessed!
God's light is my protection.
I am the reflection of God's gift.
I am safe.

God has a purpose for my life.
I help those who cannot
help themselves.

I am a role model. I get along
with others. I treat people
the way I want them to treat me.

I am full of self-confidence and self-love.
I accept myself as I am.

I can do anything my mind is set out to do.
Whatever I believe in, I can do it.

I trust myself and my decisions. I dream BIG!
I go after what I want.
I have a positive attitude.

I love to learn new things.
I enjoy sharing new ideas.
I have a great future.

I am a fighter. I am brave.
I am a survivor.

I accept myself even when I fall.
I get up and try again
and give it my all.

15

I am healthy and filled with energy.
I go beyond my expectations.

I believe in myself.
I am a winner.
1

18

I can be whatever I want to be.
I open myself up to new possibilities.

19

I am, I can, and I will.

It all begins and ends with me.

I AM...

When Shamaya Raphael was three years old, Maya always stressed the importance of her appearance. Shamaya would ask, "Mommy do I look cute?" Mommy affirmed she is a beautiful princess. But, being a princess does not only mean looking beautiful. It meant to feel beautiful as well. Mommy started teaching Maya affirmations to build her self-esteem, self-worth, and self-confidence. The Affirmations found in this book will transform the lives of children and adults. This self-help book boosts confidence, self-esteem, self-worth, and self-love. It helped Shamaya become more aware of who she is inside and out, and she hopes it will transform everyone reading this book.